Ghosts, Rogues and Highwaymen

20 Stories from British History

Geraldine McCaughrean was born in North London and has a degree in Education. She has been writing full time for many years and has won the Whitbread Award, the Guardian Children's Fiction Award, the Carnegie Medal and, most recently, the Blue Peter Book Award.

Ghosts, Rogues and Highwayman is the fourth in a series of five books which will include all 100 stories from *Britannia: 100 Great Stories from British History*.

Ghosts, Rogues and Highwaymen

20 Stories from British History

Geraldine McCaughrean
Illustrated by Richard Brassey

TED SMART

for Jess

This edition first published in Great Britain in 2002
by Dolphin paperbacks
a division of the Orion Publishing Group Ltd
Orion House
5 Upper St Martin's Lane
London   WC2H 9EA

The stories in this volume were originally published
as part of *Britannia: 100 Great Stories from British History*,
first published by Orion Children's Books in 1999.

This edition produced for
The Book People Ltd
Hall Wood Avenue,
Haydock,
St Helens WA11 9UL

A catalogue record for this book is
available from the British Library

Printed in Great Britain by
The Guernsey Press Co. Ltd, Guernsey, C. I.

ISBN   1 85881 894 X

Contents

Introduction

The period spanned by this book throws up more than its fair share of villains – from the unspeakable Witchfinder General to the murderous Master of Stair. But in among them are those loveable rogues the British relish best: the harmless, rascally moonrakers, the roguish highwayman. Perhaps at a time when plague was rife, when the very weather seemed to be rioting, when the Divinity of Kings – even the shape of the Universe – was being called into question, it is inevitable that law and order feature less than stories of villainy and suffering.

Chicken and Bacon
1626

"Knowledge is power," said Francis Bacon, and being an eloquent and sought-after lawyer, he knew the taste of both. Unfortunately, Bacon spent money as he spent words – in extravagant torrents. In order to pay his bills, he was quite prepared to prosecute former friends, marry for money, and accept bribes. It has to be said that though Bacon wrote volumes about virtue, he did not possess much himself.

His glittering legal career came to an end in the Tower of London, imprisoned for dishonesty, and though King James I generously set him free, the last five years of his life were spent writing, studying and pleading for reinstatement.

Everything interested him – from law to poetry, science to politics. And when it came to science, he did not stop short at dry theory: he believed in experimentation and irrefutable proof. Knowledge, he said, came as the fruit of experience.

Riding in a coach one bitter March day, with Dr Witherborne, the King's doctor, the two got talking about the rotting process in food.

"I have observed that the cooler the pantry, the fresher the food," mused Witherborne.

Bacon was not feeling well that day, but a sudden

idea so intrigued him that he quite forgot his aches and pains, and leapt down from the carriage. Beating on the door of a cottage at the bottom of Highgate Hill, he fetched out a timid, startled woman. "I want to buy a chicken!" demanded Bacon.

"Yes, sir! Of course, sir! Got a nice little hen-bird out back . . ." She wrung the hen's neck and brought it to him, swinging it limply by its head.

"Could you pluck it, my good woman?"

The woman plucked it, while Bacon stamped about in the garden gathering up fistfuls of snow and cramming them into the pockets of his frock coat. "And draw it?" he called. The woman pulled out the chicken's giblets and washed the carcass at the pump.

Then Bacon sat down on a stool in her cottage and began to ram handfuls of snow into the chicken.

"Are you gone entirely mad, Bacon?" enquired the King's doctor politely.

"I find myself asking," replied Bacon, grunting and red in the face with exertion, "whether snow cannot be used to preserve meat, as well as salt. What would you say?"

Excitement carried him through; he completed the stuffing. But when it was done, and the chicken sat pinkly lopsided on the table, leaking snow, Bacon found he did not feel at all well. Staring at hands blue with cold, he murmured, "I must lie down a while, Witherborne."

The doctor offered to take him home – it was only a few miles – but Bacon could not face the journey. "Take me to Arundel's house. It is only a step down the road."

The Earl of Arundel agreed, yes, of course Bacon must be put to bed in his house, and told his maid to run warming pans over the sheet in the guest room. But it had been a long while since the guest bed was slept in. The warming pan raised a gentle steam off the damp sheets, and while Bacon lay clutching his chilled stomach, the bed cooled around him.

Within a couple of days, his cold had turned to bronchitis, his bronchitis to pneumonia. He was running a temperature, alarming the maids with feverish talk of knowledge and power, chickens and immortality.

The last piece of knowledge to be grasped by the great genius of Francis Bacon was brought to him minutes before his death. It did not concern the nature of God, the afterlife or any of the usual things which prey on the minds of the dying. It concerned the well-being of a frozen chicken sitting on a plate in a pantry downstairs.

"It is not decayed one jot," Dr Witherborne whispered in his ear, and a serene smile spread across Bacon's face. He died in the powerful knowledge that refrigeration does indeed preserve food.

Francis Bacon (as well as being regularly credited with writing Shakespeare's plays for him) rose to become Lord Chancellor to King James. As a young man, he attached himself to the Earl of Essex who treated him with immense generosity, but when Essex was tried for treason, Bacon abandoned him and helped bring about his conviction. He also prosecuted his friend the Earl of Somerset for murder, rigging the evidence to get a conviction. Said to be massively arrogant and devoid of moral scruples, he was nevertheless a great thinker who wrote books on law, history, science and philosophy, and translated the Bible. His one regret when he died was having written in the English language, believing only works in Latin would survive the passage of time.

Jenny Geddes Strikes a Blow

1637

King Charles I believed that he had been placed on earth by God to rule His people. He knew he was in the right. In fact Charles did not even feel the need of a Parliament in order to rule.

John Knox believed that Jesus Christ was the only intermediary between an individual and his God. In church even a king had no higher role than his fellow men: he certainly did not have the right to set bishops in authority over the people. Knox had studied under the great preacher Calvin, and he knew he was in the right. What is more, he had utterly convinced the people of Scotland.

So, when nearly a century later, Charles I ordained that Scottish worship should fall into line with the Church of England, acknowledge him as head of the Church and submit to his bishops, Presbyterian Scotland seethed. *Bishops* dictate to Presbyterian ministers? *Bishops* lord it over Scottish con- gregations, wearing their fancy garb and offering up prayers for an English king? *Bishops* stand up in the pulpit of the High Kirk of St Giles', where John Knox had stood and preached Reformation? It seemed they must. One Sunday, the music began and the procession of ministers headed by a bishop glided serenely into position between the altar and the people.

The whole nave of St Giles' rumbled with resentful murmurings.

Jenny Geddes was just a poor market-stall holder, not a trouble-maker. But the sight of those rich, white robes encrusted with precious wire and gemstones, and the bishop's droning, patronizing sermon, put her into such a towering rage that she leapt to her feet. Snatching up the three-legged stool she had brought to sit on, she hurled it at the bishop in the pulpit – a wild, inaccurate throw – shrieking, "Ye'll nae say your mass in my lug!" The stool bounced and clattered and broke.

But nobody ever saw where it landed. For by then the kirk was in uproar. The congregation surged to its feet with a kind of angry cheer. The bishop, mouth ajar, struggling for words to condemn such blasphemy, saw a tide of angry faces, saw that the tide was rising – moving forward – coming after him! Clutching his robes in both fists, he turned to run down the pulpit steps, but already he was surrounded. Half carried, half chased, he and his fellow ministers were thrown out of the High Kirk of St Giles' like cats out of a fish shop. The Scots valued their religion above their king, and if Charles wanted to send any more bishops into Scottish kirks, then he would have to send an army first!

Soon after that, a document was drawn up entitled the "Solemn League and Covenant", plainly stating the way in which the Scottish Church should be governed. Scots flocked from far and wide to sign it – to declare themselves "Covenanters", willing to lay down their lives in defence of their religion.

CONSTANT ORAL TRADITION
AFFIRMS THAT NEAR THIS
SPOT A BRAVE SCOTCHWOMAN
JANET GEDDES ON THE 23 JULY
1637 STRUCK THE FIRST BLOW IN
THE GREAT STRUGGLE FOR
FREEDOM OF CONSCIENCE WHICH
AFTER A CONFLICT OF HALF
A CENTURY ENDED IN THE
ESTABLISHMENT OF CIVIL
AND RELIGIOUS LIBERTY

A stone set in the floor of St Giles', Edinburgh, marks the spot where Jenny Geddes is supposed to have thrown her stool. Though it is not certain the event ever took place, the legend is very popular there, since it shows the indomitable pride of the Scots, their refusal to kow-tow to English tyranny. The rising of the Covenanters meant Charles I had to raise an army. Unable to do this without the aid of government, he restored Parliament (yet again) – then found it was keener to criticize him than to fight Covenanters. In the end Charles infringed just too many laws and liberties, made too many enemies. The Puritan opposition grew in strength. Civil War broke out, ending with the death of Charles and the establishment of a Republic.

The Witch-Finder General
1646

Matthew Hopkins could barely believe his good fortune as the names poured from Elizabeth Clarke's lips. Names and confessions and a fascinating glimpse of things forbidden. Elizabeth Clarke was a witch; he had never doubted it. Was she not bent and deformed – a yammering old woman whose very face scared small children? Wringing a confession from her, he had felt the hot, mouth-drying thrill of prising open a human soul like a shellfish and exposing all the vileness inside. What a pleasure it had been to hear her damn herself with talk of "familiars" and "spells" and satanic rites! Thirty-two names she had given him. Thirty-two witches – imagine! Thirty-two fewer servants of the Devil, thanks to his energetic, brilliant interrogation of this wicked old crone.

Before she and her friends were even swinging from the gallows, Matthew Hopkins was riding north from Chelmsford to rid Norfolk and Suffolk of witches too.

The pious Protestant people of East Anglia greeted "Witch-Finder General", Matthew Hopkins, much as they would a rat-catcher. They were prepared to pay good money to be rid of the evil in their midst. Yes, they knew of an old woman who lived alone with a black cat or two and said her prayers in Latin. Yes, they had known carts stick in mud, a cow fall in the river, a

child die who had been well only days before. They gave him names by the score.

Matthew Hopkins accepted £6 from the people of Aldeburgh for cleansing the town of witches. They cheerfully pointed the accusing finger. It was not for them to enquire *who*, exactly, had designated Matthew Hopkins Witch-Finder General. It was not for them to question his motives or methods. He was doing God's work, wasn't he, rooting out servants of the Devil?

He said he carried "the Devil's list of all English witches". And besides, he had the needle. Hopkins was a pricker, and a pricker is a valuable man to have around when there are witches. No easy matter, sometimes, to find the "witch's mark" – that red, sunken place on the body which, when pricked, feels no pain. Hopkins knew where to look – the soles of the feet or the scalp of the head. Then out would come the needle – three inches of spike on a handle, like a bradawl. And in it would go, without a cry of pain from the accused.

The actual torture of a prisoner might be forbidden . . . but that was no drawback to a man gifted in the art

11

of *persuasion*. Starvation. Solitary confinement. Forcing someone to sit cross-legged for days at a time . . . there are many ways of making a person confess. In Kings Lynn they paid him £15 for the work he did.

Why, in Brandeston village, the *entire village* denounced their vicar as a witch, so how could there be any doubt? It was just a matter of obtaining a confession. So John Lowes was locked up and kept awake day and night for a week, forced hourly to run up and down his cell until he agreed to say anything. Anything. Everything. How he had bewitched cattle. How he had sunk that ship in calm weather . . . So what, if he did retract it all afterwards? These witches will say anything to save their necks . . . How those parishioners wagged their heads as Lowes was led to the gallows. *They* knew him for what he was; *they* were not going to shed any tears at the man having to read his own burial service to himself because, as a witch, he was denied a clergyman.

By the time Matthew Hopkins got to Stowmarket, his fee had gone up to £23.

In Bury St Edmunds, all told, he had sixty-eight people put to death.

His real triumph came when he hanged nineteen women in a single day.

What things they confessed to! What sensational pictures they drew – of dancing demons, Satan dressed as a bridegroom, cows jumping over stiles, men flying over weathervanes on the backs of black dogs. What a spectacle they made for the crowds to watch as they struggled with the hangman, swearing their innocence! The people of East Anglia were kept in a state of glassy-eyed hysteria, as Matthew Hopkins prowled among them, pointing the finger, jabbing with his needle.

After he retired – after that jealous wretch, John Gaule, slandered him, and his health broke down – did Hopkins lie awake at night and wonder about the pains in his chest, the blood in his lungs, about the cold sweat and colder nightmares that crawled over him? Did he wonder whose curse was gnawing on him; of those 400, which witch had done for him?

Matthew Hopkins was a self-appointed witch-finder. He and his assistants John Stearne and Goody Philips quickly got rich, preying on superstitious, vindictive people. They were helped by widespread membership of a rabid Protestant cult which prized the line in the Bible, "Thou shalt not suffer a witch to live" and thought the Devil was infiltrating the countryside with armies of witches. Civil War was raging. The Rev John Lowes had Royalist sympathies; his parishioners/accusers were mostly Puritans who hated his politics. For fourteen months, Hopkins had free rein. Then John Gaule, a vicar, wrote a pamphlet exposing him – his lack of credentials, the spring-loaded, retractable "pricker", the ease of extracting confessions from tormented prisoners. There was no scandal. Hopkins retired quietly to Essex, his fortune made, and died of tuberculosis. Another, less reliable story says that he was tried as a witch himself, put to ordeal by water, and drowned. Similar witch-hunts happened all over Europe and Russia. It has been estimated that one million innocent women died.

Cromwell and the Goosefeathers

1649

Oliver Cromwell was a man of the fens. He knew the lores and traditions of those flat, wet, wilderness lands, and he knew their uses. When he needed men to fight King Charles I, he had only to show a goosefeather to the men of the fens and they were obliged to join him – obliged by age-old tradition to offer help and protection to anyone carrying a split goosefeather.

Little by little, battle by battle, Cromwell and his Roundheads got the better of the King and his Cavaliers in a Civil War which saw the country hacked into bloody factions.

Once or twice the trick with the feather recoiled on him. At Snow Hall in Norfolk, it seemed that Cromwell had King Charles cornered, but the King's party escaped through the fens, showing a split goosefeather to the Norfolk Roundheads who barred their way. What could the sentries do? They were fenland men. They honoured the ancient symbol, and let the King slip by, though it left them in fear and trembling of their lives. What would Cromwell say when they admitted to letting the King go?

He said little. Though victory had been snatched from him, and the war prolonged by wearisome months, he listened to the sentries' explanation, took the split goosefeather from their trembling fingers and said, "Better that the King should go free than that old customs should be broken."

Of course his religious zeal gave Cromwell perfect confidence in the ultimate outcome of the war. He knew it was only a matter of time before he defeated Charles. Victory came at the battle of Naseby, and within the year the defeated Charles was brought to trial for his life.

The trial was never going to be fair, but it was no more unfair than the times decreed. Besides, only one outcome was possible in the circumstances. Charles Stewart, one-time King of England, was found guilty and condemned to death by beheading.

The night before the execution, Cromwell sat eating supper when there was a knock at the door.
It was a messenger from the King.

"His Majesty scorns to ask mercy," said the messenger, "but demands the right and privileges owing to one who presents this!" And he threw down a split goosefeather on to the table.

Even after supper had been cleared, Cromwell went on sitting at the table. All night long he sat there, twirling the broken feather between his fingers, his eyes looking unseeing into the darkness.

It snowed during the night – soft, white flakes, as though the sky were moulting, and a multitude of downy feathers fell on Whitehall, blurring the outline of the scaffold. Charles put on two shirts that morning, so that any trembling from the cold might not be mistaken for fear.

"I go from a corruptible crown to an incorruptible, where no disturbance can take place," he said, mounting the scaffold. Then he told the executioner the signal he would make when he was ready for the axe to fall, and knelt down at the block.

Afterwards, the King's remains were coffined on the spot and carried away. Cromwell went to see the body – stood for a long time holding the lid raised, gazing at his dead adversary. There was no trace of triumph in his eyes, no hatred or gloating satisfaction. There was no guilt, either. "His body was made for long life," was all he said. Then he laid a single, split, white goosefeather on the King's breast and closed the lid. His conscience was clear. After all, he had granted the King a kind of safe passage: he had set his soul free.

Cromwell and his New Model Army defeated Charles I in the Civil War of 1642-9 and established a Commonwealth, with him as Lord Protector. He was a clever statesman and military leader, but as much a dictator as any king and a dyed-in-the-wool Puritan, abolishing such jolly pastimes as dancing, the theatre and Christmas. When Charles's son, Charles II, was restored to the throne, and the Commonwealth was over and gone, Cromwell's body was made to pay for what he had done. It was dug up from Westminster Abbey and hanged from the gallows at Tyburn. The head was cut off and impaled on a pike, on the roof at Westminster Hall. Twenty years later, in a storm, it rolled down the roof and landed at the feet of a guard who took it home and hid it up his chimney. Passing from hand to hand, bought and sold like stolen goods for 250 years, it was at last presented to Cromwell's old Cambridge college and given a decent burial.

The Moonrakers

1650s

When Wiltshire wool was the finest in the world, some of the richest men in England were the wool merchants who set up business in Swindon. But they were foreigners – men from Holland and Flanders – and on spring days, when lambs were gambolling in the field, the woollenmen would sit sipping Wiltshire wine and sighing. Come autumn nights, too, when the fleeces were baled, the woollenmen still sat sadly, staring into empty glasses and sighing. They longed for a taste of home, for proper Hollands gin – but they were not prepared to pay the crippling tax that the British Government added to the price of imported liquor. A cask of "Hollands", with import duty, cost a week's profits.

And so, these men of business, and merchants and movers of goods, set about quenching their thirst. They diversified. That is to say, they opened up a new line of business. From the moonlit decks of little ships sailing up the Solent came shadowy figures to the weed-slippery coves of the Hampshire coast. They carried mysterious bundles which they hid under the stooks on haywains, and from there the cargo bumped inshore to church crypts and village lock-ups, to pigeon lofts and dry wells and disused outbuildings. Along hollow hedges and down old lead mine-shafts came casks of

Hollands gin, travelling north in a series of overnight stages, to the thirsty woollenmen of Swindon.

Don't picture a handful of dubious-looking characters with eye-patches and a beltful of pistols. These smugglers were not recruited from among rogues and vagabonds. Hundreds of ordinary people were soon employed, year in, year out, in fetching home the Hollands. For a quid of tobacco or a little brandy cask (duty-free, of course), a vicar might allow the use of his crypt or turn a blind eye to the sound of carts at midnight. For a bunch of lace, the innkeeper's wife might lay out supper after hours, and watch the wall while the "Wiltshire gentlemen" refreshed themselves on their journey. And the excisemen, though they might ride patrol, and offer rewards, and lie in ambush on moonlit nights, rarely made an arrest. Smuggling was no crime in the eyes of true-born Englishmen. This was easing the springs of contentment. This was the

occupation of gentlemen and right-thinking citizens.

Consequently, when the dewponds and duck-ponds of England greened over with summer algae, their depths often concealed a cask or two of Hollands bound for Swindon – casks which lay there for one night, then moved on northwards. One night, the smugglers of Cannings village grew over-bold, and went out when the moon was full, to the village pond, armed with rakes and an easy conscience.

"Where is it, Sam?"

"Over left of centre, Will. There, just where the moon is . . ."

Out of nowhere, the excisemen were on them, galloping up with muskets and dark lanterns and barking commands: "Stand still! His Majesty's Excise! Show your faces! Name your business!" There was an incriminating silence. "Just as I thought! Smugglers!" said the captain.

Then Jack Brown jerked his rake at the pool and began lurching from foot to foot as if he were two-parts drunk and three-parts simple. "S'a moon, maisters, that's what. Moon's falled in the pond, see maisters? Gonna rake it out an' be rich frever'n'ever!"

"Amen!" said Sam Baker, rolling his eyes and letting his hands dangle like a fool.

"Rich! Rich! Yeah! Wanna share, maisters?" asked Will recklessly. "Ye help us get her out, an' ye can 'ave a share, right enough. Must be worth plenty, woun't you say? Peece o' the moon?"

The excisemen looked at the moon's reflection in the pond. They looked at the fools on the bank splashing away with their rakes, trying to rake the moon out of the pond. "More brains in a duck egg," said the captain of the patrol. "Sergeant, let's leave these buffoons to drown themselves. Raking for the moon, indeed! They're stark mad!" And they rode off, laughing at the stupidity of Wiltshire yokels.

They should have known better. There is no such thing as a stupid Wiltshireman. Within half an hour, another three barrels of best Hollands had been dragged out of the pond and were on their way north.

For 200 years the Wiltshiremen ran Hollands gin, French brandy and tobacco, duty-free, to grateful customers. Somewhere along the way, the smugglers came by the name of Moonrakers. It was a title no right-thinking Englishman disdained to wear, a name whispered with pride and relish.

The villages of All Cannings and Bishops Cannings both lay claim to the story of the Moonrakers, but plenty of other Wiltshire villagers consider it theirs. In fact "Moonraker" has become a term to describe any Wiltshireman. In other versions, the villagers pretend to think the moon's reflection is a cheese which they want to drag out and eat. And since the story turns up in other forms and other countries – *Brer Rabbit*, for instance – it may well be a story-teller's invention. Rudyard Kipling immortalized the work of the Wiltshiremen in his poem "A Smuggler's Song" and the famous lines:

> *Five and twenty ponies*
> *Trotting through the dark –*
> *Brandy for the Parson,*
> *'Baccy for the Clerk;*
> *Laces for a lady, letters for a spy,*
> *Watch the wall, my darling, while the*
>   *Gentlemen go by!*

The Royal Oak

1650s

Charles I's son had himself crowned in Scotland, and rode south to be avenged on Cromwell for killing his father, and to take up his father's place on the English throne.

It was a misguided idea. Cromwell was ready for him. At the battle of Worcester, 4,000 died and over 7,000 more were captured within five hours. Charles Stuart was forced to flee for his life. At three in the morning, after the battle, he and a handful of supporters reached a Catholic house where they could finally snatch a bite to eat and take stock of their dire situation. Cromwell would be scouring the country for Charles – to put an end once and for all to the Stuart royal line. The King must disguise himself and get away to France.

So they buried his fine clothes in the garden and cut his long, ringleted hair short. The would-be King of England was rechristened Will Jones the woodcutter.

"Don't walk so upright and dignified," they told him, "and try to talk like a peasant."

The rain poured down all day. Charles stood dismally in a wood, with a billhook in his hand, getting drenched to the skin, while bands of Roundhead cavalrymen beat at the door of every royalist house in the Midlands.

At nine o'clock, under cover of darkness, Charles Stuart and a man called Penderel set off for Wales on foot. The old patched shoes they had given "Will Jones" were too small and the King's feet hurt. The coarse woollen stockings chafed the King's feet raw. Penderel chivvied him on to the next safe address – only to be informed that the countryside was rife with Roundheads: they must turn back. But at least the King was able to beg a pair of soft green stockings.

In wading across a stream, those green stockings filled up with sand. The King sat down, refusing to go on. Tactfully, respectfully, Penderel insisted, until the hunted King reached Boscobel House in Shropshire, and was given into the care of one Colonel Carlos with instructions to get him to the sea.

"There are Roundheads everywhere," Carlos told him. "Any minute they will come here to Boscobel, searching. It's best we hide somewhere outside."

So, provided with a ladder, a cushion and some bread and cheese, King Charles II and Colonel Carlos climbed into an oak tree. Roped with ivy, dense with leaves and peppered with acorns, the oak took the King to its noble heart. He was so exhausted that he fell asleep almost at once, his head cradled on Carlos's arm. The colonel's arm went numb; his legs roared with cramp, but he dared not move: if the King stirred in his sleep, he might easily fall off the branch and plummet to his death.

Down below, the clop of horses, the rattle of weapons announced a party of Round-heads searching the forest. Carlos prayed. The King woke and prayed, too.

"Did you see a tall man, richly arrayed – a man

running for his life, perchance?" asked a voice directly beneath the tree.

"I did so, sir!" said a girl's voice, eager and bright. "Going that way, two hours since."

The horses galloped away into the distance: the Roundheads had been sent on a false trail.

A reward of £1,000 was offered for the capture of Charles Stuart. And yet he passed safely from one household to the next and no one betrayed him. When the King expressed a longing for roast mutton, his host and hostess went out and stole a sheep so as to grant the King his wish: Charles cut and cooked the chops himself, finding the novelty of it hilarious. On the road south, an innkeeper called out: "God bless your Majesty wherever you go!"

Later on, "Will Jones the woodcutter" was transformed into "Will Jackson the servant" and had to share a horse with a maid. Awe-struck at having to wrap her arms around the King's royal person, Mistress Lane frequently forgot to treat him like a scullion. Once, they rode directly into the middle of a troop of Roundheads . . . but passed unnoticed.

Once on the journey, "Will Jackson" was told to wind the spit over the kitchen fire, to brown the meat. In his ignorance, he wound the handle the wrong way. "What manner of man are you that you don't know how to wind up a jack?" demanded the cook.

Charles thought quickly. "Where I

come from we can't afford
to eat roast meat," he said
piteously. "And when we
do, there's no jack to cook
it on."

When the horse cast a
shoe, they had to stop at a
forge and listen meekly
while the blacksmith
talked on and on about
"that rogue Charles
Stuart". In fact Charles

Stuart even joined in, agreeing with the smith.

A ship lay at Shoreham bound for France. As Charles, exhausted and careworn, climbed gingerly into a sailor's canvas hammock, the ship's captain rushed below decks. "I know very well who you are!" he said. The King, too weary to rise, boggled over the side of the hammock at the captain, who fell on his knees. "And I would lay down my life to set your Majesty safe in France!"

Lying in that hammock, listening to the creak of the ship's timbers, his cabin rocking gently around him, Charles pondered how to reward such people – all those brave, loyal souls who had been willing to risk their lives and lands to help a defeated man escape his enemies. One day he would return to England and occupy his rightful place as king. No more need for hiding like an acorn buried in the ground. He would flourish like a mighty oak, giving shelter to his people.

When the story of Charles's escape became known, the acorns of the oak tree at Boscobel were planted far and wide. From the acorns grew oaks, and by every oak an alehouse or inn. On Oak-Apple Day, the King's health was drunk at those inns. Long after Cromwell and his Common-wealth were gone and forgotten, the Royal Oaks flourished. And even after the oaks perished, the story survived.

During Oliver Cromwell's Commonwealth, most of the rural festivals and semi-pagan rites were banned – along with such harmless pleasures as dancing, theatre and Christmas. All the old May-Day celebrations were axed, many of which involved a pre-Christian reverence for oak trees. The story of the Royal Oak gave the perfect excuse to revive some of these customs. Oak-Apple Day (29 May and Charles Stuart's birthday) is known, in different parts, as Arbor Tree Day, Shit-Sack Day, Pinch-Bum Day, Oak and Nettle Day ... and not all have much or anything to do with Charles's lucky escape. Wearing a sprig of oak leaves on Oak-Apple Day is seen, however, as a declaration in favour of monarchy.

The Tyburn Dancer

1660s

The driver banged on the coach roof. "You ladies may want to draw the blinds! We are coming to Hounslow Heath, and the gibbets are not a pretty sight to look on!"

Even with the blinds closed, the passengers on the post-coach could hear the creak of ropes, the jingling of chains, as hanged men swung in the breeze. Hounslow Heath was forested with gibbets, for any highwayman hanged at Tyburn had his body returned to the scene of his crime and hung up in chains . . . and the heath was a favourite haunt of such men.

"Foul beasts," said Lady Cynthia, fanning herself furiously.

Lord Babbacombe patted her hand. "Destroy 'em like the vermin they are, I say!"

"Isn't there something rather romantic about them?" said Lady Dorothea. "Living by moonlight, on the brink of disaster?"

"Not when they strangle a defenceless woman for the crucifix round her neck," said her husband. "That's what happened last week, close by here."

Lady Cynthia whimpered.

"Let 'em all dance at a rope's end, I say!" declared Lord Babbacombe.

As if in answer, a voice just beyond the closed blinds

cried, "Stand and deliver!"

The coach lurched to a halt. The driver swore. Lady Cynthia swooned clean away, and Lord Babbacombe tried to hide underneath her spreading skirts. Dorothea's husband – a man of considerable wealth – hurried to prime his pistol, but the priming pin fell into the dark bottom of the coach and rattled out of sight.

The door opened, and there stood a man, prodigiously tall in his tricorn hat, one foot up on the running board and a pistol in each hand.

"Permit me to introduce myself. Claude Duval, native of France and gentleman of the English countryside. Your money, if you please, sirs!" Then he saw Dorothea. "If your hand is already spoken for, lady, I must settle for your jewels," he said, and somehow succeeded in bowing, without his pistols so much as wavering.

"Sir, my heart belongs to my husband here, but your manners commend you," said Dorothea looking him boldly in the eye. "I have heard your name spoken in the most exulted circles, Monsieur, though I had hoped never to meet you myself."

The eyebrows above the mask rose a little, and the mouth below it smiled. "Madam, pray do not fear for your safety. Your beauty is such that I could ask nothing more precious from you than the honour of a dance."

Dorothea did not turn to her husband for advice: her eyes remained fixed fast on Duval. "But where is your music, Monsieur?" she asked.

He made a flamboyant gesture with one pistol. "We have the music of the spheres, do we not, Lady?"

"In that case, I shall pay your toll, Monsieur Duval."

There was no moon: highwaymen do not work by moonlight. But the stars shone on that stately pavane. The men by the coach watched open-mouthed as the two figures paced out a dance in time to Duval's humming.

"They say a woman was murdered last week, by one of you 'gentlemen', for the sake of the crucifix around her throat," said Dorothea pertly.

"Do not bless him with the name of 'gentleman'," said Duval. "The dogs who do such things are beneath contempt, and I will shoot him myself if he ever crosses

my path! May the lady's ghost hang round his neck till doomsday."

"And where, pray, will your ghost be seen after you are dead, Monsieur Duval?"

"Why, dancing on Hounslow Heath, God willing, with a woman of grace and spirit!"

"Just so long as you never dance on Tyburn Tree," she said, and for the first time that night a shiver of clammy fright went through her.

When the dance ended, Claude Duval took the gems from around Lady Cynthia's neck, a watch and purse from the man hiding under her skirts. He asked of Dorothea's husband just £100 – a tenth of what he might have demanded. But from his dancing partner he took nothing. "I consider myself in your debt, Lady," he said, thrusting the pistols back into his waistband and bowing with a flourish of his tricorn. "My life is far sweeter for meeting you tonight!" Then he whistled for his horse, mounted and rode away.

Afterwards, Dorothea thought of him often and wistfully, though her husband never mentioned the incident, or allowed her to speak of it. When she opened the newspaper one morning and read that Duval was betrayed, arrested, condemned to hang, her own words clanged in her head like a funeral bell: "Just so long as you never dance on Tyburn Tree."

Screwing up her courage, Dorothea hired a chaise to take her to Tyburn. But as she approached the place of public execution, she tapped on the coach roof and called for it to stop. All around the gallows washed a sea of satin and lace, a raft of elegant hats, the susurration of a hundred sighs. Half the ladies in London seemed to have come to make their farewells to the French gallant.

Later, when the notorious Claude Duval had kicked out his last dance at the end of the hangman's rope, been hung up in chains, cut down and buried, a headstone appeared mysteriously to mark the place. It read, "Here lies Claude Duval. If you are a man, beware your purse, if a woman, your heart. He has made havoc of both."

Unknown to Dorothea, her husband had repaid his own debt of honour for the gentlemanly fashion in which Duval had treated both his wife and his wallet.

Most highwaymen (such as Dick Turpin) were brutal thugs involved in a variety of petty crime, including highway robbery and murder. But there were some "gentlemen-of-the-road" who became popular heroes, because they displayed courage or panache. The fact that they preyed on the very rich made ordinary people like rather than condemn them. The Bishop of Raphoe was shot and killed on Hounslow Heath – not *by* a highwayman, but in his guise as part-time highwayman. It was even seen as a kind of honour to be robbed by a notorious highwayman. One renowned statesman actually wrote to his attacker assuring him that he held no grudge for his accidental wounding. Claude Duval came to England at the time of Charles II's restoration to the throne, a courtier in the household of the Duke of Richmond: a born gentleman, even if his chosen career was in crime. He was arrested while drunk, and hanged at the age of just twenty-seven. The famous epitaph on his grave at Covent Garden no longer exists.

The Village that Chose to Die
1665

The first instinct was to run: to pack up bags and bedding and children into a cart and to get away. And when the first cases of plague hit Eyam Village, some did go. There were a few deaths in the autumn, then a season of happiness, when the village seemed to have been spared. In the spring, it came back: the Black Death – moving through Eyam like a stray cat scratching at every door to be let in.

The people went along to the church that day with their minds full of plans and fears. Where should they go? To which relative? Not the plague-stricken London, that was sure. They had only half an ear to lend William Mompesson, their priest. But then they realized what he was saying.

"The plague travels about the country in the blood of those fleeing it. In trying to get away, folk take a death sentence to another community of souls, condemning them too, to die. When a fire breaks out, we protect the houses round about by making a firebreak and starving the fire of new timber. That's what we must do here. As we are Christians, we must be prepared to die in order that others may live. For Christ says, 'Greater love hath no man than this . . .'"

Stunned, the people of Eyam gaped at him. He made it sound so simple. Isolate the disease so that the disease might die out. He was asking them to stay in Eyam, to make no move to get away; to cut themselves off and let the plague burn itself out within the available people – within their children, their loved ones, themselves. Three hundred and fifty people, waiting for an inevitable and terrible death. And yet the man had such an air of certainty. Amid all the confusion and terror, he knew what to do. They must simply stop struggling – deliver themselves into the hands of God and the plague.

Of course they did everything within their power to avoid infection. Some smoked pipes all day long, some wore charms and bunches of herbs, some carried nosegays to keep off the stench of death. But the people

of Eyam followed the instructions of their priest. As travellers neared the village a sentry would call out, "Go back! We have the plague in Eyam. Go round us, and remember us in your prayers!"

Supplies of food and quicklime and tobacco and so forth were brought to the boundary stone or the well and left where the payment lay, in vinegar-washed, sterile coins. The curious came for a while, to shout questions across the river. But soon no one came. For all Eyam knew, the rest of the world had died.

If William Mompesson thought that God would spare the people because of their selflessness, he was mistaken. One by one they fell ill, each one suffering days of tormenting pain and wretchedness while neighbours watched from a distance, much as people might watch a rabid dog die in the street. The lucky ones died suddenly, after a few hours of raging fever. Sooner than move bodies through the streets, families dug graves in their gardens, ready for when they were too ill to dig them. Mrs Hancock buried her husband, three sons and three daughters in the field beside her house, within the space of eight days.

The church was locked – too good a breeding ground for the disease – but William Mompesson kept on holding services, out in the open air, under a scorching summer sky endlessly smutted with flies and the ash of fumigating fires. He had raised this dwindling little congregation of patient saints halfway to heaven. William Mompesson had done that much for them, and that was more than any surgeon or apothecary could have done.

On 7 September 1665, George Viccars, a tailor in Eyam, in the Peak District, received a parcel of cloth from London, and in it a cloud of fleas, thought to be the source of the epidemic. He was first to die. Three-quarters of the population of Eyam died of bubonic plague within a year. Unlike other "plague villages" which were totally abandoned during the Black Death of the fourteenth century, Eyam survives to the present day. Meanwhile, in London, nearly 70,000 deaths were attributed to the Great Plague.

The Great Fire of London

1666

It was nobody's doing, nobody's fault. Suddenly, at two in the morning of Sunday, 2 September, a pile of firewood stacked against the wall of the baker's shop in Pudding Lane burst into flames. (It was the back wall of the oven, and so of course the bricks grew hot.) Mr Faryner the baker woke to find the room full of smoke and, when he reached the head of the stairs, could see at once there was no escaping that way. The whole of the ground floor was alight.

"Wife! Wife! Wake up unless you want to burn in your bed!"

They climbed out of a dormer window in the roof and spread-eagled themselves against the roof tiles, feeling for the gutter with their feet. The air was full of smuts and smoke. At the window the maid sobbed: "I can't! I can't do it, Mr Faryner! I'll fall! It's too high!"

There was no turning back for her – no reasoning with her as she grew more and more hysterical. The baker pressed on, balancing his way along the guttering, while down in the street a crowd of neighbours gathered, stupid with sleep. They watched till the screaming figure of the maid fell back from the window, replaced by leaping spectres of flame.

For an hour the baker's shop alone burned – a bad blaze but not the first in a city of wooden and wattle houses. Neighbours fearing for their own property fetched out buckets of water, but there was no organized attempt to isolate the fire. A brisk wind was blowing. Above the heads of those watching, burning straws and cinders and ash floated in search of kindling.

By morning, the whole street was ablaze.

Lord Mayor Thomas Bludworth was a dithering, indecisive man. He would not order the pulling down of undamaged shops and houses to make a firebreak. "Who will pay for the rebuilding?" he asked querulously. For hours he hesitated, while the fire leapt from roof to rooftop and strung the narrow streets with yellow buntings of flame.

Cellars packed with fuel, barrels of pitch, winter supplies of tallow exploded, throwing burning clods of wattle high into the air and showering the streets with tiles. Families in the path of the fire began to bundle their belongings together into chests and bags and to move their children out of doors. Here and there, gangs of men banded together to fight the fire, but all they had were buckets of water and hand-held squirts. They might as well have spat on the flames. King Charles II, looking out over London, saw the daylight choked by a rising mass of black smoke. "Tell the Lord Mayor he may have all the soldiers he needs!"

"How did it begin?" was all the Lord Mayor wanted to know. "Who's to blame?"

"Foreigners!" people told him. "Fire raisers! Revolutionaries!"

Mr Faryner the baker was summoned to tell what he knew of the fire. Anxious that no one should blame him, he remembered mysterious, suspicious circumstances – the fire starting far from the bread oven, for no good reason. And it had spread so fast and so far! There must have been arsonists operating all over the city!

People powerless to stop the fire turned their energies to finding the culprits. A Frenchman was knocked down with an iron bar for the crime of being foreign. A woman holding her apron gathered up in front of her was set upon by a mob screaming, "Look! Look! She has fireballs hidden in her apron! She's carrying fireballs! Arsonist!" The woman sprawled senseless in the open drain, and a dozen fluffy yellow chicks scattered out of her apron and ran cheeping hither and thither.

At last, the Lord Mayor gave permission for a firebreak to be made, and soldiers with billhooks began pulling apart whole streets of houses, while the householders screamed prayers and abuse and clutched their children close or dragged their furniture clear of the tumbling masonry. But it was too late. The fire leapt their firebreak, a surf of sparks spilling onwards to set alight wash-lines, hay-carts and more thatches.

Down at the river, the watermen had mustered every watertight boat and barge in the city and were busy evacuating families and goods down-river. The river was a red glare, the smoke an artificial night, but the watermen were pitiless in demanding their fee. As the hours passed, and they found they had more trade than they could handle, they demanded higher and higher sums. Huge purses of money changed hands so that a dresser and a harpsichord should float with their owners downstream, out of danger. Already there were tables and benches afloat on the tide, safer in the water than out of it.

Crowds jostled at the waterside for a chance to board, children up to their knees in mud, women balancing on jetties and landing stages, men haggling and swearing. In among them, pick-pockets were lifting a fortune in watches and silk handkerchiefs, an unattended valise here, there an unguarded roll of cutlery.

The goldsmiths and silversmiths of the city converged on the Tower of London, to deposit their valuables in the stone vaults and impregnable dungeons of the ancient fortress. But would even the Tower keep out the fire now shredding to rags the London skyline? Church spires were toppling like trees, stone buildings crazing, crumbling, crumpling, their stones bursting like bombs.

The booksellers of London chose St Paul's Cathedral as a safe place for their stock, for it was built in stone and lead and bronze – not kindling like the houses which jostled round it.

Many people also looked for sanctuary in the various churches, only to be harangued by preachers wild-eyed with zeal. "This is the judgement of the Lord! Yea, He hath poured out brimstone on the heads of the unrighteous!" They were out on the streets, too, the evangelists, bellowing in the ears of the milling crowds, their spittle gleaming in the firelight: "God sendeth down destruction on this City of Sin, on this generation of sinners!"

Certainly hell did seem to have risen close to the surface of the world that day. In places the ground was too hot to walk on, and the air seared nose and throat and lungs. Rats and mice driven from the burning buildings squealed like demons along the streets. At one time, an area two miles long and one mile wide was alight and burning. The army was blowing up buildings with gunpowder now, adding to the din.

At eight o'clock on Tuesday night, a cry went up which turned the booksellers' hearts to printer's pulp. St Paul's was burning. Lead streamed molten out of its roof, pouring down in cataracts of incandescent silver, splashing on to the faces of the saints and madonnas, obliterating the bronzes on the floor: "Here lies the body of . . ." Into the vaults it poured, making a bonfire of the books and pamphlets and maps and Bibles in a blaze which leapt back up to the carved angels on the hammer beams. The great bells, set swinging and ringing by the hot updraught, began to lose their shape, to soften and bow, to sag, to melt in brilliant torrents.

In the Inner Temple, the beautiful, ancient buildings wavered in the heat-warped air – a golden rain of sparks falling on their roofs. A sailor called Richard Rowe, accustomed to going aloft in rigging, clambered on to the roof of the great hall, as lawyers in wigs and gowns gaped up at him, clutching precious documents. All he had was a pillow, and as he straddled the roof ridge, he beat at flames which scuttled like rats across the tiles.

The great fire had reached the limit of its strength. The explosions had finally starved it of new food. Now, here, at the Inner Temple, it lost the fight against a single man and a pillow. Richard Rowe saved the great hall, to the choking cheers of lawyers and judges, clerks and secretaries. As he sat there astride the roof, all he could see as far as the levelled horizon was smoking devastation.

Outside London, in the parks, 100,000 people huddled bewildered and homeless amid the few worldly goods they had managed to save – a cradle, a wheelbarrow, a sedan chair. The King organized relief supplies of food to be fetched in from the countryside, and personally administered the billeting of the homeless in pubs, inns and churches. Before long, he was commissioning brave new buildings, planning a more open, elegant city than the one which had grown up hugger-mugger, in squalor and overcrowded filth, over 1,000 years. But those who had lost their homes simply roamed about the ruins, picking over the ashes of their houses, counting the cost.

OLD ST. PAUL'S

In four days, 2–5 September 1666, 456 acres of London burned down in the Great Fire; 13,200 houses were destroyed and 87 churches. St Paul's, the Royal Exchange, the Custom House, Newgate Gaol and the Guildhall were all lost, though the destruction enabled such architects as Sir Christopher Wren to prove their genius afterwards. Samuel Pepys, in his renowned diary, recounted his own experience of the fire.

Yet despite the size of the disaster, only six people died. The previous year, 70,000 had died in the Great Plague of London. By destroying the clutter of close-packed housing, the Great Fire made London a safer, healthier place to live.

Colonel Blood Steals the Crown Jewels

1671

One day, while Mr Talbot Edwards, the deputy keeper, and his wife were taking tea, a clergyman and his wife called at the Tower and asked if they might view the Crown Jewels.

It was not an unusual request. Old Mr Edwards was accustomed to giving his little informative talk as he displayed the royal sceptre, the sword of state, the jewelled gauntlets and coronets and, of course, the coronation crown. He had been doing it for years.

Such an agreeable couple, Mr and Mrs Edwards agreed afterwards – especially when the gentleman called a week later with a pair of gloves for Mrs Edwards "in gratitude for her great kindness". Seeing the pair of pistols hanging on the wall of the apartment, the clergyman admired them so much that he begged to buy them, then and there!

The friendship flourished. So it seemed the most natural thing in the world that their clergyman friend should bring along two acquaintances – visitors to London – to view the Royal Regalia. That was the morning of 9 May.

Beginning his well-worn talk, Mr Edwards laid out the gems and collars, diadems and weapons on the table in the Jewel Room. "And this, gentlemen, is the coronet worn by . . ."

Suddenly, Talbot Edwards – who was past eighty – found himself enveloped in darkness – a cloak over his head, a wooden bung pushed into his mouth to gag him.

"Give us the crown, the orb and the sceptre and no one will get hurt!" the clergyman hissed in the old man's ear.

But Edwards took his responsibilities to heart. The shame of losing the treasures in his charge to a band of tricksters and brigands was more than he could bear. He began to struggle and moan and kick and wrench himself to and fro in their grasp. They struck him once with a wooden mallet, then when he still struggled, struck him again and again.

"Keep him quiet, can't you?" Colonel Blood snarled.

They stabbed Edwards to silence him.

Colonel Blood beat the crown of England out of shape and crammed it under his cloak. Another man dropped the orb down the front of his baggy breeches. But the sceptre of state was too long to fit up a sleeve or down a trouser leg. They flung it on the table and began to file it in two.

Then a sharp whistle from their look-out on the floor below warned of danger: visitors for the Edwardses! The keeper's son and son-in-law were coming up the stairs! Edwards' visitors opened the door of the apartment to be met by a stampede of masked men, a volley of shouts and swearwords. They were shoved aside, but quickly realized what was happening, crying, "Stop the thieves!"

There was a warder on the drawbridge. Running

towards the commotion, he was confronted by the small black circle of Blood's pistol barrel pointing in his face. He saw the hammer lift, the spark flash, then fear swallowed him up in a black unconsciousness he mistook for death. The shot had missed, but Blood and his cronies were through the iron gate and running for the tethered horses.

Talbot Edwards' son put on such a sprint that he crashed into Blood and bowled him off his feet. The crown clattered to the ground, gems and pearls jarred from their settings and rolled away like so many pebbles.

The news was shouted from street to street clear across London: "Have you heard? Someone's tried to steal the Crown Jewels! . . . A band of brigands! . . . They broke the sceptre! . . . They murdered the guards! . . . But they've been caught! . . . And now Blood is refusing to speak to anyone but the King of England himself!"

To everyone's surprise, King Charles II granted Blood an audience.

But did the colonel throw himself on the King's mercy? Did he plead insanity or swear that he had been forced to commit the crime against his will? Far from it.

"Yes, I did it!" said Blood. "I would never deny it to save my life. It was my plan and it was only by the greatest bad luck that it failed. I'm no more sorry than I was when I kidnapped the Duke of Ormonde! No more sorry than when I lay in hiding at Battersea and aimed a gun at you, Charles Stuart, as you went down to bathe in the river."

The audacity of the man, the knowledge he had

come so close to being assassinated all but silenced the King. "What stopped you shooting me?" he asked at last.

"My heart was checked by an awe of majesty which caused me to spare the King's life," said Blood. "I shall never name my accomplices. If any of us die, the rest are sworn to be avenged for that death. But if your Majesty were to spare us, the pardoned men would doubtless be ready to do the King great service. We have already proved our daring, you'll agree."

"Take them back to the Tower," said the King, and his court waited, with horrid glee, to see what terrible

retribution would overtake the villainous, the shameless, the arrogant Colonel Blood. As if the King could be intimidated by empty threats! As if the King would use the services of such unmitigated rogues!

Within days, Blood was free. Not only free, but his estates were restored to him along with an income of £500 a year. Talbot Edwards lived, but received almost nothing for his loyal service – a pittance in comparison with the rewards Blood received from the King.

So did the King so much admire daring and audacity that he was ready to let an unrepentant criminal go free? Or was he scared of revenge attacks following Blood's death? Or did Blood and the King share some secret which placed the lout beyond reach of the law? Rumour spread that he had done the King some huge favour so murderous and wicked that he held the King in the palm of his hand, free to say what he liked, do what he pleased, rather than swinging at the end of a hangman's rope.

COLONEL BLOOD

By the end of the Civil War, Thomas Blood, Cromwellian, had risen to the rank of colonel. But with the restoration of the King, he lost his estates in Ireland and was reduced to poverty. He was involved in every uprising and act of insurrection to spring up in England or Scotland. The ballads sung about him, the personal recollections of those who met him do not paint a lovable, raffish rascal but a dangerous, amoral terrorist and hired assassin. So why his immunity from the law?

It is thought that his patron, the Duke of Buckingham, may have been behind the kidnapping of the Duke of Ormonde. Now Buckingham was one of the King's favourites. So did Blood simply shelter under Buckingham's coat tails?

Run for Your Life!

1685

When King James II put down rebellion in the West Country, he wanted to make sure that no one ever dared to question his kingship again. So he employed Judge Jeffreys to make an example of the rebels, and the judge went to it with a will. He hanged men by the hundred.

Young Hughie was famous. Throughout Somerset he was renowned for the speed and distance he could run. Champion of a hundred races, Hughie of Westonzoyland was both sprinter and marathon runner and could outpace running dogs and outstay an army horse.

"They say you can run, boy," said Judge Jeffreys, supercilious under his black cap.

"I can."

"And I say you can't. A wager on it. What do you say?"

"I have nothing to wager," said Hughie, wary of the gleam in the judge's eye.

"Wouldn't you wager your *life*, boy, that you could outrun a runner of mine?"

"That I would!" Hughie was over-quick to accept the bet. There among the numberless nooses, the trees dangling with hanged men, the muttered prayers of Catholic priests over Protestant prisoners, he grabbed at the chance to live. He knew he could outrun any man in the county. To win his life he was ready to run as he had never run before.

"Then fetch out a horse and tie him to the stirrup!" commanded the judge. "If he tires before the horse, he shall hang. If the horse tires first, I shall rethink my verdict." And before Hughie could draw a good, deep breath, someone slapped the horse across the rump and it sprang forward.

The animal was unnerved by seeing movement in the corner of his eye, by the noise in his swivelling ear of a man's laboured breathing. At first the two of them jostled one another – man and horse, horse and man. The jeering spectators fully expected to see Hughie dragged to his death.

But Hughie timed his strides by the hoofbeats, stretched his gait to match the sway and thrust of the big fetlocks, and soon the pair were running side by side, leaving their captors staring after them. In a panic, soldiers mounted up to give chase and keep the prisoner in sight.

Across the green curves of Somerset, Hughie and the stallion ran; across the green swelling hills, across pillaged farms, past burned buildings and the wreckage of gun carriages. Horse ran and man ran, and if once the pace slowed, there were plenty of shouts from

behind to spur on the frightened beast.

In time the horse became accustomed to his running-mate, and Hughie, far from hating the beast, found more in common with its pounding, pungent bulk than with the men hooting and whooping behind. He made of himself a machine, his legs the mill-paddles, the ground the water driving them. "I will run for my life or die running," he told himself.

He thought of Anne, his sweetheart, her sadness at thinking him dead, her joy in finding him alive, his life won back like a trophy. *She* was the trophy at the end of the race. *She* was the goal which kept him running when his legs burned like twin fuses and his lungs were two tattered flags, when his head rolled on his shoulder heavy as a cannonball.

The stallion had no such goal. That is why, in the end, he tired. After three hours of running, his breath broke in his windpipe and his sweating flanks heaved. He slowed to a canter, to a trot, to a walk, then pitched down so that Hughie fell on top of him.

To Hughie's surprise the noise, swelling louder and louder as his pursuers caught up, was of breathless cheering. Miles earlier, the jeering had given way to admiration – wonder, even – at the strength and courage of a young man who could outrun a horse.

They took off their hats in salute to him. They carried him back to the judge eagerly, with the news loud in their mouths: "He did it, sir! He did it! The horse tired first! He did it!"

The news of the rebels' defeat by the King's army reached Westonzoyland fast. So did the story of the race: man against horse, horse against man, and how their Hughie had won it. At the village inn they drank a toast to their champion runner: the man who could win any race in the county and who had given them back their pride as West Countrymen, even in defeat. They rattled at Anne's shutters and crowned her with may, because until Hughie came home, his sweetheart was the next best person to crown. She came down to them and danced, in celebration.

Then the news arrived that Hughie was hanged.

The judge had never meant to keep his side of the bet. The race had been, for him, no more than a moment's entertainment in a long tedious day. In Westonzoyland, joy turned to outrage, then to gnawing, blistering despair. While village thoughts turned again to killing and rebellion and revenge, Anne slipped quietly away.

A ghost runs now across the Summer Land: not a boy's athletic ghost timing its paces to the beat of ghostly hoofbeats, but a little pattering ghost wearing a crown of may. Because Anne drowned herself at the news of her sweetheart's death. Now her ghost gasps and sobs and stumbles breathlessly on, everlastingly trying to outrun her grief.

JUDGE JEFFREYS

On 11 June 1685, the Duke of Monmouth, illegitimate son of Charles II, landed at Lyme Regis, hopeful of wresting the crown from his uncle, King James II. Over 4,000 West Countrymen mustered to his Protestant cause. For a month – the so-called "Duking Days" – these rebels held Somerset, and Monmouth was proclaimed King in Taunton market-place. But when James brought his full wrath to bear, his army easily defeated the rebels at the battle of Sedgemoor. Monmouth was captured, and cravenly and unsuccessfully begged for his life, even at the cost of turning Catholic. Meanwhile the notoriously harsh Judge Jeffreys was sent to Taunton to try captured rebels. His "Bloody Assize", estimated to have hanged 200 men, transported 800 more to the West Indies and whipped and fined countless others. His barbarism inflicted wounds on the West Country for which neither he nor James, his paymaster, were ever forgiven.

Glencoe
1692

The thing was to get it over and done with, then put it out of mind. The thing was to say: these are not people, these are MacDonalds. War hardens a man, and after a few years in the army, he can stomach almost anything. It is a lot to ask of a man, even so, to eat another man's food, to sleep under his roof, to accept his hospitality, then to murder him.

Still, King William was determined to be rid of the "Auld Fox" MacIan and the rest of the MacDonald clan once and for all.

So we were billeted on them, with the excuse that the garrison at Fort William was too overcrowded to hold us. As we marched into the glen – 120 men of the Earl of Argyll's Highland Regiment – McIan's sons appeared and asked if we came as friends or foe. "As friends," said Glenlyon. "As friends".

For fifteen days we lived in their poor wee houses, in that great valley called Glencoe, where a river of wind flows always cold, and where the snow fortifies the mountains into castles high as the sky. The Master of Stair had said it must be done in winter, because it was the one time the Highlanders could not elude us and carry their wives, children and cattle to the mountains.

They did not suspect anything. After all, the "Auld Fox" had pledged his allegiance to King William, so he thought he had nothing to fear, even though we were Campbells. (The Campbells and MacDonalds have hated each other for as long as I can remember; that's why Stair chose us for the job.) Also, we had accepted MacIan's hospitality, and that should have guaranteed our goodwill. That's the unwritten law of the Highlands.

So we played cards with the MacDonalds, we drank with them, exchanged stories with them. We sat down to suppers cooked by the women, and our knuckles knocked against their knuckles as we reached into the same bowl for our food. The children tugged at our uniforms, wanting to be sung a song. Their mothers hushed them to bed: "Do nae fash the officer: he needs his sleep."

But there wasn't to be any sleep. At nightfall we were summoned outside and given our orders by Glenlyon. We did not go back in to our beds. When they saw us checking our muskets, the MacIan boys asked: "What's happening?" But Glenlyon only laughed and told them we were going out next day to tackle a local band of robbers.

The time was set for five in the morning, when the clansmen would be asleep or just stirring. So we waited, watching the moon move over the glen through tangles of snow-cloud, a thistledown of snow blowing.

Come five o'clock we went to it. Bayonets fixed. No shot to be fired, that was the order. But some of us were jumpy – or squeamish – and we used our guns. The MacDonalds would have woken anyway, I know. The screaming would have woken them soon enough.

We killed more than thirty. You wouldn't think that would take long. And yet the screaming seemed to go on for an eternity. Sometimes I hear it still in my sleep. Men, women, children. Everyone under seventy years, the order said, and don't trouble the Governor with prisoners. If they locked the doors against us, we set the house alight and burned it down, with the people inside. Women. Children. Fourteen in one house.

In the confusion, some got away, out of the village. It didn't matter. It's so cold up there, the snow lay so deep, and them in their shirts for sleeping, barefoot, without cloak or blanket: we knew they would freeze to death on the mountainsides.

In the house where I had stayed, nine clansmen were gathered round the morning fire when we went in shooting. Four died where they sat. We split up and went after the women, the bairns, the old folk. I came face-to-face with the owner of the house, the one whose knuckles had brushed mine as I reached for bread at supper. Odd how, in all the din – the smashing of furniture, the screaming, the shooting, the curses – there seemed nothing between us but silence. A blanket of silence. Then the man said, "Let me die in the open air, man, no under ma ain roof."

I had steeled myself against the usual things: "Let me live. Spare my wife. Pity the bairns." This seemed such a small thing to ask: "Let me die in the open air."

"For your bread which I have eaten," I said, "I will." So we pushed him out of doors with our musket butts, and he stood there in the dark, his face underlit by the snow. We levelled our muskets.

Then he up with his plaid – that piece of tartan they all wear for a cloak – and threw it in our faces and ran. We fired after him, but the snow swallowed him up. Maybe he lived. Maybe he froze to death, being without his plaid. Part of me hopes he got clear.

But Glenlyon saw it happen and came down on us raging. "There's two more run into the forest yonder!" he bellowed at me. "Get after them and finish them both!"

From the edge of the wood I could hear them crashing through the deadwood; clods of snow slumped down from the trees, showing the way they had gone. Besides, I could see their footsteps in the snow – one set deep, one set so small and light that it scarcely dented the snow. Pretty soon the snowy trees swallowed up the roar of burning buildings behind me, the crack of muskets. It was silent where I found them: a silent, grey, hollow world pillared with bare tree trunks. A woman and a child, too exhausted to go any

further, clung to one another gasping, their breath curling into the air like musket smoke. I fired once, reloaded, fired a second time.

Twigs and snow tumbled down on to me from where the musket balls had holed the leaf canopy overhead. The woman looked at me, her hand clamped over the child's mouth to keep him from screaming. We neither of us said one word.

Then I pulled the shawl from round her shoulders, turned on my heel and headed back. On the way, Providence set a wolf in my path, and I killed it and daubed the shawl with blood. I had to have something to show Glenlyon.

All in all it's not a night's work I'm proud of. If you ask me, I'd say the killing was folly as well as a sin. When word spread, even the sassenachs* pitied the MacDonalds, whereas up till then Highlander and Lowlander had scorned one another. We Campbells were shamed by it. That's my opinion.

I don't tell people I was there. I don't say, "I was at Glencoe." You only have to mention the word and men shudder. I shudder: almost as if the snow blew inside me that night, and lodged where it's never going to thaw. At five in the morning, I lie awake and shiver.

*Sassenach (literally Saxon) is an abusive term for a Lowlander or non-Scot.

CAPTAIN CAMPBELL

The Glencoe massacre was an atrocity brought about by one man's obsessive loathing of the MacDonald clan: Secretary of State for Scotland, Sir John Dalrymple, Master of Stair. Stair had already persuaded King William to put to the sword anyone who would not pledge allegiance to the crown. But MacIan *had* signed for the MacDonalds. Even so, Stair succeeded in sending 120 Campbells, commanded by Captain Campbell Glenlyon, to massacre the clan. More than thirty were killed, another 300 fled into the blizzard. Chieftain MacIan was shot in bed by a man he had invited to dine; his wife died of her injuries. His sons escaped. The legend of the woman and child was added later – echo of Snow White. Another legend tells of the Campbells led astray by mountain spirits on the way home.

The British public were so shocked by the massacre that Stair was shunned for a time . . . but was ultimately made an earl. Politically, the massacre was a disastrous move, unifying Highlanders and Lowlanders in bitter hatred of the English.

The Lighthouse and the Storm

1703

Henry Winstanley designed playing cards and lived in the depths of the country, miles from the sea. So he was not the most obvious contender for the task of building a lighthouse. But whereas others tried and gave up, Winstanley maintained it was perfectly possible and that he was the man to do it. In 1696 he mustered carpenters and engineers and, with his meticulous plans rolled up under his arm, sailed out to the Eddystone Rock to start work.

Ever since vessels first set sail from the English coast, the Eddystone Rock had been a menace to sailors. On a calm sunny day, it looked like nothing – a jag of rock jutting high enough out of the sea for gulls to perch. But in a fog, or when the waves ran so high as to hide it altogether, the Eddystone Rock could rip the keel out of sloop or merchantman or fishing smack. Countless sailors had drowned in the waters around it, and their sunken ships were now crewed by conger eels and shoals of ghost-white cod.

The task would have been hard enough, even under ideal conditions trying to work on a weed-slippery, spray-wet rock while battered by wind and sea, trying to sink foundations sufficiently deep to raise up an indestructible tower twenty-five metres tall. As it was, Winstanley had to contend with dangers of a different sort.

Press gangs roaming the inns and kitchens of the south coast in search of able-bodied men saw work begin on the Eddystone Rock and rubbed their hands with glee. When a press-gang paid a visit there, the builders would have nowhere to run. Winstanley's workmen were coshed and bound and carried off to serve as seamen in the Royal Navy – pressed men – leaving nothing but a scattering of tools and timber. Winstanley recruited fresh men, but there was an understandable shortage of volunteers.

During construction, Winstanley often chose to sleep on site rather than waste time coming ashore. One night, he and his builders were woken by the rhythmic splash of oars, the thud of a rowing boat pulling alongside the rock. French troops, in cockaded hats and with muskets primed, came scrambling over the moonlit reef, barking unintelligible commands at the sleepy, bewildered English. For a few minutes it seemed as if the entire construction team would be murdered where they huddled.

Winstanley tried to reason with them: "Look, I know we're at war, your country and mine. But you French *need* this lighthouse just as much as the English! Does the rock sink only British ships? Does it drown only English seamen?"

Despite his protests, Winstanley's builders were stripped naked and cast adrift in a rowing boat. But at least *they* stood on English soil next day, whereas Winstanley found himself in a French prison. The Admiralty were incensed. They arranged for a mutual exchange of prisoners – and put Winstanley back to work building the Eddystone Light.

At last a core of stone was grafted on to the rock, and on to that a wooden tower, with a windowed chamber at the summit where hung a kind of three-tiered chandelier, crammed with tallow candles. The night those candles were first lit, Winstanley's face glowed almost as bright with pride in a job well done.

"It'll never stand up!" people said.

Praise for Winstanley's handsome lighthouse was guarded. A great many people said it would fall down within days. "I only wish," Winstanley answered them, "that I may be in the lighthouse in circumstances that will test its strength to the utmost."

November 1703 ended amid filthy weather. Then,

on the twenty-sixth, a gale struck the south of England more ferocious than any recorded before or since. People woke with the impression that the world was coming to an end, and when they looked out of their windows, they were certain of it.

In London 700 boats and barges were ripped off their moorings and piled up in matchwood mountains against the bridges. The roofs were ripped off houses like so many fish-scales, whirling the contents into the sky, pelting those outdoors with furniture, masonry and tiles, cats and food and roofbeams. Churches collapsed as though built of biscuit crumbs. A flood tide, inflated by the wind, swept up the river and swamped the City, washing over the venerable stone floors of Westminster Hall, setting afloat the bodies of those killed in the maelstrom. Off the coast, three warships foundered with 1,500 men aboard, and 200 sailors were glimpsed, stranded and drowning on the Goodwin Sands.

The face of the English countryside was scarred by those two days of the Great Storm. Whole villages foundered, whole copses were uprooted, barns folded flat. At least 8,000 people died, though the chaos and horror were so great that no true count was ever made. Tens of thousands were injured.

In the depths of the Essex countryside, in the parish of Littlebury, one house stood pretty much unscathed. Hardly any damage befell the home of Henry Winstanley, engraver, inventor, designer of playing cards and lighthouses. A small silver replica of the Eddystone Lighthouse fell from a table: that is all.

Winstanley was not home to see it, however. He was out on the Eddystone Rock, visiting his lighthouse which had recently been increased in height to thirty-seven metres.

On the morning of 28 November, the Great Storm subsided. When the people of Plymouth looked out to sea, they could see the horizon once more, though the sea was still white with rollers. They looked towards the Eddystone Light, fully expecting to see it wrecked, its pulleys and winches snapped off like tree branches, its lattice windows smashed. But they saw none of this. In fact, they saw nothing. Not a trace. Every stone and plank and nail and candle of the Eddystone Lighthouse had disappeared, as surely as if it had never existed. And with it had gone its creator.

A new light was built five years later, and stood for almost fifty years before catching fire. The lead roof, in melting, poured down in a glittering torrent – directly into the gaping mouth of the lighthouse keeper. His slow, agonizing death is commemorated in the local museum by the lead ingot which solidified inside his stomach. But of Winstanley, nothing remains but rumours mouthed by silent conger eels and ghost-white cod.

The Great Storm of 1703 was a hurricane which originated in North America, crossed the Atlantic and carved a path across Europe before spending itself in the Siberian wastes. In Britain it caused an estimated £4 million worth of damage – the equivalent of billions nowadays; 400 windmills were destroyed and hundreds and thousands of cattle and sheep drowned in the floods. The writer, Daniel Defoe, wrote of the scene in London: "no pen can describe it, no tongue can express it, no thought conceive it, unless some of those who were in the extremity of it." The present Eddystone Lighthouse, built in 1882, is the fourth construction on the rock.

The Bubble Bursts
1720

Strange and far-off lands have always held most magic for those who will never go there. In the early days of the eighteenth century, South America was imagined as a faery mound shot through with precious ore. It had gold, and everyone dreams of laying hands on gold.

The South Sea Company *did* exist: it was not imaginary, nor was it set up with a view to defrauding anyone. Real ships *did* sail, from time to time, between England and South America. There *was* some money to be made. But that has nothing to do with what happened in the City of London during the winter of 1719.

Rumours spread that British cargoes landing in South America would be exchanged for outlandish quantities of gold and silver. Investors in the South Sea Company stood to increase their money a hundredfold. Here was no shady, crooked enterprise: the Government itself held South Sea Company stock! Here was an opportunity for people of all kinds to get rich fast. Even when war broke out, ending trade agreements, people went on believing the South Sea Company would somehow continue to bring home vessels wallowing under tons of gold.

There was a stampede to invest. The value of shares soared: money was pouring in – not from South

America but from eager investors all over England. A kind of investment fever broke out, which saw all manner of people thrusting their savings at the company's brokers, begging to be allowed to share in the bonanza. A few cautious voices warned against it: no company could or would pay profits of the kind talked of.

But the directors of the South Sea Company realized just how deep they could dip into the pockets of the gullible. When the share price began to drop, and uneasy crowds gathered outside the offices, well-dressed men strolled among them still beaming with confidence. They had been in Peru and Chile. They had seen the gold ingots piled up in the streets like bricks. Any fool could see how much those shares would soon be worth!

Fools there were in plenty. The share prices soared again. New shares were released – at a price. Hurry, hurry, hurry. Only the quick will get rich . . .

'Change Alley in the City of London was a scrum of people, from dawn till dusk, buying shares from trestle tables. A blizzard of application forms! Quill pens were at a premium; so was ink and somewhere flat to write. A man bent double by disease was charging a penny for the use of his back as a table. He went home with a big bag of pennies – solid, round, brown pennies – and kept them under his bed. A frenzy of greed had gripped the country – a kind of trance which no amount of shouting or cool reason could penetrate.

Those with wit enough saw the game for exactly what it was – a hysterical dash to buy worthless pieces of paper for absurd sums of money. Those with no conscience set up joint stock companies of their own, and issued shares, selling them in 'Change Alley. Why invest in South American gold when you can invest in a process to make sea water drinkable? Or in a perpetual motion machine? Or in re-floating treasure ships wrecked off the coast of Ireland? Why not put your money into making planks from sawdust or importing donkeys from Spain? Fortunes were to be made overnight: did it not say so on the handbills? One day a notice went up offering shares in the ultimate deceit:

> A Company for Carrying on an
> Undertaking of Great Advantage,
> But Nobody to Know What It Is.

The shares sold. Share-fever was such that people could hardly help themselves any more.

To those who did not have £100 to invest right away, came a new temptation: £100-shares in return for a down-payment of £2. Only £2 down and you could be holding a share document worth £100, then and there! Who could fail to be tempted? In the course of a day, 1,000 of these shares were issued, in a room crammed from door to window with pushing, impatient people, all chinking their golden guineas. At the end of the day, the office was locked. The broker washed the ink from his fingers, emptied the day's takings into a carpet bag, and caught the boat for France. He had invested one day of his time and earned £2,000.

Very soon afterwards, Mr Knight, treasurer of the South Sea Company, packed a bag, disguised himself, and also made his way to the Thames. A vessel was waiting to take him to Calais. The value of South Sea shares was dropping. Nothing could hide the truth this time. An airy idea had been inflated to impossible size, and now the South Sea Bubble had burst. There was nothing in it – nothing but hot air and greedy hopes.

Thousands were ruined, their savings gone, their dreams sunk in the South Sea. It almost brought down the Government. It threatened to topple the King from his throne. Public despair was so great that the sighs must have been heard as far away as South America.

It was Dean Swift, author of *Gulliver's Travels*, who coined the name "bubble" for the kind of shady business which thrives by attracting absurd amounts of investment. It still happens today. Sir Robert Walpole, foreseeing the grief to come, had actually begun moves to ban bubble companies before the South Sea Bubble burst, but had been powerless to enforce the ban. The entire national mood was soured by the affair. A period followed of bitter cynicism in all aspects of public life.

Makers and Breakers
1730s

In the bright, large-windowed cottage in Bury, the weavers worked away on their looms, passing the woof through the weft, tapping each strand into place, their cloth growing inch by laborious inch. And as they worked, they talked of John Kay and his invention.

"Looms twice the width of these . . ."

"Double the quantity in a working day!"

"And better quality, they say!"

But their tone was not full of admiration. The flying shuttle made a weaver's task easier and produced better, broader woollen cloth, but they did not want to handle one, to master the magic of threading and throwing the ingenious shuttle.

"Should not be allowed."

"Canna be left to go on."

"Must be stopped."

"Putting skilled men out of work!"

And the mood of seething resentment came bubbling to the boil. Then, when all the useful daylight was gone and all that remained were warps and wefts of moonbeams, the weavers and their neighbours converged on Kay's house and attacked. They broke all his windows.

He was baffled, bruised and bewildered. "Why can they not see? This is their future! This is for their good!"

But the weavers hated him. They looked around them and saw all the old ways dying out, the woollen trade becoming an empire in the hands of a few wealthy industrialists, its workers forced to work harder, longer, for less. That shuttle would take food out of their children's mouths. That was how they saw it.

It was just the same when Kay moved away to Colchester – then to Leeds. Oh, his flying shuttle caught on (it was too good an invention not to) but the manufacturers who used it did not pay him anything, behaving as if they had invented it themselves.

When he started up an engineering business, the mobs again gathered to throw bricks through the windows, smash his looms. Lonely and dejected, he went back to his home town of Bury, where he lay awake nights wondering what he had ever done for these people to hate him so much. "Because a thing is new must it be bad?"

One day, the mob surrounded his house. He could hear them jeering and swearing, racketing about, their women cursing, the children bright-eyed at the prospect of destruction, excitement, violence. John Kay apologized to the friends who were visiting him. "I hope nothing unpleasant will spoil our . . ."

A shoulder thudded against the door. A window caved in, in an explosion of breaking glass. The mob poured in, like the sea into a foundering ship. John tried to save his latest models, his books, his few possessions, but saw them sunk beneath a flood of flying fists, kicking clogs, jostling shawls and wooden clubs. The satisfying sound of splintering wood made these people deaf to reason. A mob has no ears.

He fled upstairs, where his friends had already had the good sense to hide. But the mob's leader broke off and looked around. "Let us find Kay. Where is Kay?"

Kay's guests flapped open a folded woollen sheet and threw it over their friend. Then before John could protest, they bundled him up into a shuttle-shape parcel and, lifting him between them, galloped down the stairs. Passing for looters robbing the house, they got Kay away unharmed – though not undamaged.

He was a bitter man. Desperate to earn a living, he left England for France, but did no better there. Just once, he came back, to seek justice against those mill owners who had stolen his invention. He got none. Those opportunists soured him far more than the ignorant louts who had almost killed him. For the manufacturers had known just what they were doing when they tricked him out of his percentage. Besides, the wreckers – those frightened vandals who had wanted to dam the tide of progress – would quickly be swept away by it. Within a few generations, they would be living huddled in urban slums, working on deafening machines for twelve hours a day, their children crawling up and down beneath the looms, their lives reduced to figures in a ledger: profit and loss. Theirs was the loss; theirs and John Kay's. He died destitute in France.

JOHN KAY

James Hargreaves met the same reaction with his spinning jenny, Samuel Crompton with his spinning mule. When Richard Arkwright was developing his machine, superstitious neighbours complained they heard the noise of "the Devil tuning his bagpipes, and Arkwright dancing to the music". But from such inventions sprang the Industrial Revolution, transforming England's landscape, its economy, its whole social structure for ever. For a century, Progress did battle with those it was putting out of work. In 1811, a group calling themselves "Luddites" attacked stocking-making machines, power looms and shearing machines. In the countryside, "Captain Swing's" men broke up the threshing machines which deprived them of vital winter work. These were times of bread riots, enclosures, dispossessions, protest, suffering. The Government's only solution was to send in the troops.

"Charlie Is My Darling"
1746

Prince Charles Edward, son of the exiled James Stuart III, landed at Eriskay determined to raise a rebellion and restore his father to his rightful position: King of England and Scotland. His Scottish supporters – Jacobites – came to greet him. But they watched appalled as the prince's troops came ashore. Where were the French armies that had been promised? How were they supposed to topple King George II from the throne with this pocket army? "You must go home, your Highness," they said.

"Home? I am come home!" declared the prince.

His youth, his energy won over the hard men of the glens. As the song runs:

> *They've left their bonnie Hieland hills,*
> *Their wives and bairnies dear,*
> *To draw a sword for Scotland's Lord,*
> * the young chevalier.*
> *Oh! Charlie is my darling, the young chevalier!*

At first they carried the day entirely, captured Edinburgh and took control of the borderlands. They had forced their way as far south as Derby before they fully grasped how incompetent their "Bonnie Prince Charlie" was. Did he really think he could take and hold London with an army of 5,000 men? They insisted he turn back. Pettish and sulking, Charles grudgingly agreed. In the meantime, the Duke of Cumberland was marching to intercept the rebels.

On 16 April 1746 he cut them off at Culloden Moor, and shot the heart out of the Jacobites. Afterwards he slaughtered their women and children too, winning himself the name "Butcher Cumberland". But the Culloden massacre lit such a fire of hatred that the Highlanders' love for their bonnie prince burned all the brighter. He was all they had left, and they guarded him like a treasure. King George offered £30,000 for the capture of the "Young Pretender", and yet no one informed on him. It was as if mists and heather had swallowed him up.

For five months, the fleeing Prince Charlie was passed from hiding place to hiding place, from caves to cellars, fed on the meagre supplies of his supporters. Told of the reward on his head, Charles grinned. "Then I offer £30 for the head of George II!"

The Kennedy brothers, wild and shaggy as Aberdeen bullocks, robbed a Hanoverian general of his baggage – all to provide the bonnie prince with a fresh suit of clothes.

When the redcoats swarmed in like red ants from all sides and not a rat could have crept away unnoticed, one of his bodyguards said, "Lend me your wig and cloak, sire. I will lead them off." Roderick MacKenzie went out into the open, showed himself and ran. He fetched after him horsemen, foot-soldiers, and such a hue and cry as the Highlands had rarely seen. They shot him down in Glen Moriston, and as he fell he shouted, "You have killed your prince!" The head was dispatched to London and put on public display – to show what became of ambitious usurpers. A one-time servant of Charles's went along – whether to grieve or simply to stare, no one knows. But in his astonishment he exclaimed aloud: 'That's no Charlie!" It was four days before the English troops discovered their mistake – and by that time Charlie himself was heading for the safety of the Hebrides.

No sooner had he put to sea than a storm hammered on the little boat and drove it sixty miles in ten pitch-black hours. Every moment, the men aboard thought to be hurled against rocks, shipwrecked on one of the islands invisible in the dark. But when dawn crawled in under the pall of black cloud, they spotted Benbecula, and were able to pull ashore. While the storm raged on, the prince took up "royal residence" in a doorless cow-house, with a rag of sailcloth for a blanket and nothing to eat but oatmeal and stolen beef.

From Benbecula, he set sail for Stornaway, but was driven ashore on Glass Island, where the people were hostile: he had to pretend to be a shipwrecked merchant. In Stornaway, one of the servants in the party got drunk and boasted wildly that he knew how the prince was going to get to France: that called for a change of plan. Putting in once more at Glass, the party was attacked and had to row on, without food or fresh water, for two days.

Spotted by an English man-of-war, the rowers bent their backs over the oars, rowing till the breath foamed through their gritted teeth. "I'll be sunk sooner than be taken," vowed the prince. Then the wind dropped, the warship was becalmed, and the oarsmen sculled out of sight of English telescopes. "It's clear," said Charles Edward, "I was not designed to die by weapon or water."

But when his friend Clanranald found him on the island of South Uist, the fugitive prince had been reduced to living in a hovel, on a diet of crabs, haggard by sickness and hunger, dressed in filthy rags. It was decided he must be got away to Skye.

So it was that the bonnie prince met Flora of the clan MacDonald, who lived by the Uist seashore. Her mother, Lady MacDonald, lived on Skye, which gave Flora the perfect excuse for making the voyage there.

When Flora entered the hut where the prince was hiding, she carried under her arm a bundle of clothes which she told him to put on: a flowery linen dress and a deep-hooded bonnet. Bonnie Charlie became "Betty Burke", and "a very old, muckle ill-shaken-up wife",

by all accounts, striding out with his skirt in his fists, towards the rowing boat on the beach. As the little boat, carrying Flora, "Betty Burke" and three kinsmen, rolled ashore over the Skye surf, a detachment of militiamen came pelting down the beach to seize them. "Put out again! Pull away!" cried Neil MacDonald.

Flash. Flash. The flash of the muskets reached them before the noise. *Crack. Crack.* Musket balls dug tussocks of spray out of the water. "I beg you, Miss Flora, lie down in the bottom of the boat or you may be hit!" said the prince.

"I shall not, unless you do so yourself, sir," replied Flora.

"Me? I was not designed to die, either by . . ."

"Then I shall not, sir." They argued briefly, while the musket balls kicked splinters out of the boat's side. In the end, the prince had to agree to lie alongside her, while the oarsmen heaved away, and the waves rose up between guns and boat.

At long last they succeeded in landing Bonnie Prince Charlie on Skye – though truly it was no safer a place than any of the others; his life was still in hourly danger. He made a very poor woman, by all accounts. "Your enemies call you the 'Pretender'," joked one friend, "but you are the worst I ever saw!" "Betty" lifted her skirts too high when they forded one stream, and let her petticoats trail in the water at the next one. Passers-by stared at her, housemaids fled her. It was finally decided that "she" would be safer dressed as a man.

And so it was to a Scotsman, dressed in traditional tartan coat and waistcoat, kilt, wig and bonnet that Flora MacDonald said farewell. The militia were closing in; cordons were thrown across the countryside like nets to catch salmon. And yet the prince was still smiling when she parted from him, still confident that he would reach France and come back one day as king. It was that certainty which made his supporters believe in him when all hope seemed gone. But it was their selfless bravery which saved Charles's skin and wrapped him round in the myth of the "bold young chevalier".

When he finally reached France, the French king offered Charles a pension but asked him to leave: peace between England and France depended on it. Surly and resentful, Charles refused, demanding money and troops to mount a fresh invasion. He had to be arrested and forcibly removed from France. In his wandering exile, he became an alcoholic, self-pitying brute who beat his mistress, neglected his daughter and, in old age, married a teenage German princess who soon left him. Before he died, the Stuart claim to the throne was a lost cause.

Flora MacDonald was arrested and taken to London. To her astonishment, she found herself acclaimed a celebrity. She later married a kinsman, Allan MacDonald, and emigrated to America.

"Give Us Back Our Eleven Days!"

1751

Everyone knows that there are 365 days in a year. By 1752, nearly everyone knew why: because it takes 365 days for the earth to circle the sun once.

But astronomy, though it deals with such vastnesses as space and time, is an exact science. The cleverest of astronomers had already worked out that it took precisely 365 days 5 hours 48 minutes and 49 seconds – which is exact, but harder to remember. Also, calendars are incapable of dealing in hours and minutes and seconds.

If left uncorrected, century by century, a gap would develop between the seasonal year and the calendar – summer would fall in spring, winter in the autumn.

The Romans had found the solution centuries before – the leap year – and in 1582 the Pope had adjusted his calendar to match that of the Caesars. England, however, had not. In 1752 Parliament decided to accept the New Style Calendar. It almost solved the problem. Only eleven days were left – the accumulation of 1,500 years of sloppy time-keeping. The only tiny adjustment which still remained was to change 3 September to 14 September, and England and Europe could start again, level.

Say, "Time" to an astronomer, and he sees planets swinging through aeons of silent space.

Say "Time" to a mathematician and he sees a column of figures.

But say "Time" to ordinary, uneducated people who can neither read nor add up and have no interest in astronomy, and they see a collection of minutes with birth at one end and death at the other. The Bible speaks of three score years and ten allotted by God to Man. But precious few people lived to seventy in 1751, and death lurked in ambush round every corner. Suddenly it was announced that 3 September had become 14 September, and all they could see was that they were eleven days closer to their deaths.

Eleven sweet days had been sliced out of their lives; eleven days in which to earn money to feed their children, eleven days to share with their families before they died. It was as if they had gone to sleep and woken up eleven days later. They were convinced they had been robbed: the Great Time Robbery. No matter what the clever, educated people said – "All right for them; they live longer than us!" – the poor, unlettered, uninformed common people did not listen. Panic made them deaf. They poured on to the streets, rioting and yelling, "Give us back our eleven days! Give us back our eleven days!"

The Church might have soothed them. But churchmen (who tend to deplore change) dug in their heels and complained that the religious festivals were fixed by God and that Parliament could not slide them about like so many pieces on a chessboard. "We shall abide by the old ways!" they said, and clung doggedly and unhelpfully to their old calendars. Anything sooner than conform to a popish one. There was only one thing for the Government to do: wait for the outrage to burn itself out, for the protests to fizzle out, and for the eleven days to be forgotten.

Time, after all, is a great healer.

LORD
CHESTERFIELD

The Julian Calendar, adopted by Julius Caesar in 46 BC, was reformed in 1582 by Pope Gregory XIII: 5 October became 15 October. Italy, France, Spain and Portugal accepted this, but England and Russia (disinclined to do anything at the suggestion of a Pope) did not. Two hundred years later, Europe and England were operating eleven days apart, and the 4th Earl of Chesterfield took it upon himself to put matters right. He published articles, then drew up a bill to put it through Parliament. Not only was 3 September to become 14 September, New Year's Day – formerly 25 March – was now to be 1 January. Chesterfield never foresaw what a furore he would cause. You would expect the hundredth year of every century to be a leap year. But, to keep the New Style Calendar accurate, only one century in four follows this rule.

Slave in a Free Country
1763-1765

"Shipped by the grace of God in good order and well conditioned, 200 slaves marked and numbered . . . God send the good ship to her desired port safely. Amen."

So read the bill of lading on the day 200 (or 300 or 500) men, women and children were herded aboard a ship, branded with hot irons, manacled and kept in order with whips and boiling water. This was the slave trade, and until 200 years ago, it was thought of as any other trade. The Africans carried off by force from their homelands to work as slaves on the cotton and sugar plantations of America and the Caribbean were, in law, "goods and chattels" to be bought and sold like livestock. Such big profits came from the plantations and from the slave trade itself that few questioned the cruelty, the downright sin of enslaving fellow human beings.

Black faces were a common sight in London in the eighteenth century. West Indian merchants would bring with them their household servants. The London newspapers often carried advertisements for runaway slaves, offering a reward for their return. So it was not the novelty of seeing a Negro which stopped Granville Sharp in his tracks that day. It was the desperate state of the young man.

He had a bloody rag tied round his head and was

feeling his way along the railings of Mincing Lane, knees bent, back rounded, jaw sagging with misery. The curly black hair above the bandage was crisply matted with blood.

"Who are you, sir? You need help. What has happened to you? I was on my way to visit my brother – he's a doctor. Won't you let me take you to him?"

The man's head rolled on his shoulders. He was close to unconsciousness. "Jonathan Strong, sir . . . my name. My master . . . my master . . ."

Granville's brother took one look and said, "He must be got to St Bartholomew's or he won't last."

On the way to the hospital, they listened, in incoherent snatches, to Strong's story. He was the slave of a Barbados lawyer called David Lisle who had returned to live in London. Lisle had, in a fit of rage, smashed his pistol down repeatedly over Strong's head. Then, finding he had as good as blinded the man, he had pushed him out of doors as being of no further use.

For days Jonathan Strong, his skull fractured, hung between life and death. It was four months before he was able to leave hospital. All this while, the Sharp brothers visited him, and afterwards found him a proper, paying job. He was very happy and undyingly grateful.

But two years later, Jonathan was walking down a London street when a shout made him turn. There, like a scene from his worst dream, stood Lisle, red-faced with fury, pointing his finger at Strong and shouting, "Stop that man! Escaped slave!" A brief scuffle, and Strong was seized; people turned aside to avoid the unpleasantness.

Not so Granville Sharp. When Strong got word to him, Sharp went in high dudgeon to the Lord Mayor's office, and took out a summons against Lisle for detaining Jonathan without a warrant.

It was not that Lisle wanted his slave back for his own use. Seeing his slave was fit to work again – his "damaged property" mended – Lisle promptly "sold" Strong to a Jamaican planter. He shook hands on the deal, at least, though the planter would not part with hard cash until his purchase was aboard ship.

That is why it was the captain of the ship who arrived at court on the day of the Lord Mayor's decision. He had come to collect his cargo.

"It seems to me," said the Lord Mayor querulously, "that the lad has not stolen anything, and is not guilty of any offence. He is therefore at liberty to go where he pleases."

Granville Sharp raised both fists in triumph and his face broke into a grin. But not Strong's. "What's the matter, Jonathan? You're free! Didn't you hear?"

Strong shook his head sadly. "If you think that, sir, you know little of my master."

And he was right. No sooner did he step outside into the street than the sea captain grabbed him by the arm: "You're coming with me, piccaninny."

"Sir! I charge you for an assault!" Sharp's cheeks were flushed and his white lace stock rose and fell as he struggled to master his anger. The captain's hand slid off Jonathan's arm. "I want no trouble, me," he muttered.

Hotly indignant, Sharp strode home, Jonathan following after him with a hasty skip and a jump. While he was in Sharp's company, he was safe; no one dared touch him. And that was almost as good a feeling as being a free man!

The lawyers all told Granville Sharp that, in law, Jonathan was not a man but a "chattel". They said there was no chance of winning any court case. Granville was outraged. Where was the justice in that? So he set about studying the law himself, to find if it were really true. And he published what he discovered:

"There is no law to justify . . . the servitude of any man in England."

Soon everyone was discussing it. At dinner tables up and down the land, families argued and took sides:

"I'll tell you what freedom means – the freedom of an Englishman to trade in slaves, without these meddling do-gooders interfering!"

"Oh, but tolerance and liberty, my dear! They've

always been at the backbone of England's greatness! How can there be slaves *in England*? Surely, in England . . ."

Meanwhile, the wheels of law slowly turned. Lisle brought a lawsuit against Granville Sharp. Being a lawyer, he won, too. Triple damages were awarded against Granville. Law, it seemed, had decided that Jonathan Strong was *not* a free man. He was a slave. And that made him the property of Lisle to do with as he liked.

The judgement caused a stir. Granville Sharp was the grandson of a bishop, not to mention a true Good Samaritan. What he had done, he had done out of kindness and Christian charity. And did English law favour *Lisle*? Lisle the brute? Lisle the lawyer? Surely that could not be right?

When, soon after, an almost identical case arose (concerning an escaped slave, James Somersett, wrestled off the London streets and sold back into slavery), the case of Jonathan Strong had so changed public opinion that this time the judge was ready to create legal history.

"As soon as a Negro comes into England, he becomes free," he declared as he gave judgement. The escaped slave left the court a free man.

But it was a judgement made too late to save Jonathan Strong. He was "property" once more: a chattel to be shipped in chains, flogged, forced to work for nothing for the rest of his natural life. Every crusade leaves behind its casualties. Jonathan was not the first, nor the last. He was simply the one whose face haunted Granville's dreams after he saw his friend herded aboard ship for Jamaica and clapped in the hold with the rest of the cargo.

Slavery was far from over. Campaigners such as Thomas Clarkson and William Wilberforce gradually nudged the public conscience awake until, in 1807, the slave trade was finally abolished for ever by English law. This did not stop the thriving traffic in slaves, though; it was simply taken up by pirates and freebooters. For fifty years the suffering grew worse, not better. But the long humanitarian climb had begun, its ladder resting squarely on the shoulders of Jonathan Strong.

Mary's Bible
1804

There was a knock, and Mr Edwards went to the door. It was late for callers, and he was surprised to find a young girl on his doorstep. Her clothes were covered in grass and her hems were black. She looked exhausted. Mr Edwards thought she might be going to ask for money as she thrust a money-box at him.

"Mr Edwards, sir? My name is Mary Jones and I've come from Abergynolwyn. Your friend Mr Hughes sent me. I've been saving up, you see. Are there any left? He said they might all be gone!"

Mr Edwards looked up and down the street for signs of a cart. "You have come all the way from Abergynolwyn today? How did you get here?"

"I walked. I'm good at walking. I walk to school every day and home again."

"But it must be twenty-five miles, child! You must be worn out – famished! Come in, come in!"

As she ate supper, the girl explained in breathless, excitable Welsh, how she had come to buy a Bible with the pennies she had saved.

"Oh, but Mary, do you read English well enough to read the Bible?"

"Oh, not an *English* Bible," Mary said. "I've come to buy a Welsh one."

"Oh, but Mary! Did Mr Hughes not explain? The Bible in English you might just afford, but in Welsh?

Welsh editions are fearfully costly."

"That's why it has taken me so long to save up," said Mary patiently. "I knitted socks to sell at market. I helped with the harvest. I did gardening and washing for the neighbours . . . The village helped, too, of course: they gave the last shilling. So it only took me six years."

Mr Edwards was astounded. He gazed at this small, solemn, brown-eyed girl. "And do you mean to say you have worked for six years and come all this way to Bala, just to have a Welsh Bible of your own?"

"It's all I have ever wanted," she said simply. "Ever since the village got a school and I learned to read . . . Do you think there will be one left?"

The supplies of Welsh Bibles were indeed strictly limited. They arrived a few at a time, at the house of a local minister, the Reverend Thomas Charles, and quickly sold out – to wealthy householders and clergymen and schools. There was just one left when Mary and Mr Edwards reached the minister's house. The two men watched Mary Jones run her fingers over the tooled binding, the marbled end pages, the maze of Welsh words, then fold it to her chest in blissful delight. A moment later she said, "I must be going. I've twenty-five miles to go by nightfall. It will be easier going back," she explained. "I don't have all that money to carry, and I can always stop along the way and read my Bible."

The Reverend Charles could not get it out of his mind – that young girl's heroic endeavour, her single-minded determination. It thrilled and delighted him . . . and at the same time it enraged him. No one should have to scrimp and save and work and wait six years then walk twenty-five miles to own a Bible in their own language!

At the next conference he went to in London, he

stood up and told Mary's story.

"Inspiring!" said the people who heard it. "Marvellous! Charming!"

"Yes, but wrong," said the Reverend Charles. "A Bible should not be a luxury, whatever your language. It should be affordable to everyone, rich or poor, Welsh or English."

"No matter what language they speak!" cried a fervent voice from the back of the hall. "So let's do something about it! God has shown us our duty through this child!"

A clamour of boots hammered on the hall floor like a roll of divine thunder.

Out of that evening, the British and Foreign Bible Society was formed – a society which still exists today to make sure the Bible is affordable and available to no matter who, no matter where. And Mary Jones was the cause of it all. It was as if her determination and perseverance had been large enough to inspire a thousand others to do as she had done and to make the impossible happen.

The British and Foreign Bible Society was founded in 1804, with the Reverend Thomas Charles of Bala a founder member. It is now a member of the United Bible Societies which has made the Bible accessible to people in over 200 countries. The Bible has been translated into more than 2,100 languages and dialects. No one has ever been able to trace Mary Jones. Poor rural families left little documentary record, and the girl concerned may well have been renamed for the sake of simplicity and Welshness. It does not seem likely that a Welsh minister would have made up the whole story, just to sway feelings at a public meeting. Someone somewhere may, all unknowing, own the very Bible Mary saved up and walked so far to buy.

England Expects
1805

The sniper among the crew of the *Redoubtable* was sent aloft into the rigging as soon as the fleet took up battle formation. The French and Spanish ships of the combined fleet were a magnificent sight, stringing out into a huge crescent – the cupped hand which would seize England for Emperor Napoleon Bonaparte. Nothing stood in Napoleon's way but this last great sea battle. Trafalgar, it would be called, after the nearby Spanish headland.

Through his spyglass, the French sniper saw the flagship, *Victory*, and a tingling shiver ran through him. Nelson's ship! Heart of the English fleet. Within its soaring wooden walls rode the commander-in-chief on whom the English pinned all their hopes: the famous admiral who suffered seasickness when he put to sea!

Soon the British fleet would also be stringing out into a crescent opposite the combined fleet, and the two lines of ships would blast relentlessly away at each other with cannon fire until one side or other could take no more. The sniper breathed a prayer for his ship's safe deliverance.

But the British fleet did not string out. It came steadily on – two clusters of warships sailing head-on into the crescent. It was madness! Without turning broadside to the enemy, they could not fire their guns! With a roar like a dragon waking, the French and

Spanish cannon opened fire. For twenty minutes they spat venom at the *Victory* and the huddle of ships beyond her, and yet the British fleet did not turn to fire a single shot in return! The signal flags with which Nelson had addressed his sailors – "England expects that every man will do his duty" – soon hung in smoke-soiled rags and tatters, the rigging in knotty festoons.

But at the end of that twenty minutes, the *Victory* was passing close by the stern of Villeneuve's flagship, the *Bucentaure*, gun doors open, cannon primed. When at last she fired such a broadside into the Bucentaure, 400 men fell instantly to the deck, dead or wounded.

Suddenly the English ships were rubbing sides with the French and Spanish ones, firing into them from such close range that great gaping holes were blasted in the wood walls, and buckled cannon rolled over into the sea. Villeneuve had never encountered these tactics, and by the time he realized that Nelson had rewritten the manual of sea-going warfare, it was too late to think up counter measures. The English ships grappled with the combined fleet, and English sailors swarmed over on to French and Spanish decks. The battle of Trafalgar was to begin with a surprise and end in hand-to-hand combat.

Up on his masthead perch, the French sniper watched in horror the rack of the combined fleet. He saw twelve good ships sunk or disabled, saw his own ship grappled and pulled close to the *Victory*. *Redoubtable* heeled and lurched over. The top of the mizzen mast was caught in the broken and flying rigging of the *Victory* and, for a while, the two ships clung to each other like wrestlers in a fight to the death.

And there he was on the quarter-deck: Nelson! It had to be him! His uniform did not give him away, for he was not wearing all the gold braid and epaulettes of dress uniform, but he was wearing the four medals of knighthood which his adoring country had awarded him. And it was on those medals that the sniper took aim.

Such a tiny man – small as Napoleon himself! Skinny, too. Only one arm, one eye and built like a sickly stray kitten. How had this man cast such a vast shadow over the destiny of his country? The sniper's hands shook with excitement, but he aimed true.

He could at least make Horatio Nelson pay for thwarting Bonaparte. The flash of the musket blinded him for a moment, then the smoke cleared, and he saw Nelson on his knees – a frozen tableau of officers watching their commander fall. Nelson slumped over on to his side.

Someone shouted, "There he is!"

The Frenchman in the rigging of the *Redoubtable* put a hand to his chest in wonderment. Could he be feeling the little Englishman's pain! Was this the penance for taking a hero's life? To feel his death pangs? Then the sniper looked down and understood. He saw the English sharp-shooter, musket smoking. As he fell out of the rigging, he thought: "*Enfin. Je l'ai tué.*" At least I killed him.

Nelson was carried gently below decks. Officers clamoured and crowded round, calling for the ship's surgeon, telling themselves that he was not badly hurt . . . But Horatio Nelson knew he was dying. Inside his head images of his past life were flooding in like the sea into a holed ship: the coldness of the surgeon's knife that day his arm was amputated; the glitter of flying stone fragments before his right eye was blinded. The polar bear loomed up again over him which, at sixteen, he had fought on the Arctic pack-ice. The parsonage where he was born. The face of Lady Hamilton, passion of his life. One kiss from her soft lips and the pain in his side would surely cease . . .

"Kiss me, Hardy," said Nelson, to the officer crouching beside him. They puzzled over it a long while after. Had he perhaps said, "Kismet – (Fate) – Hardy"? They scribbled them down, these last, strange words of a famous man. "Have them take care of

Lady Hamilton. Without my protection, I fear . . ." Hardy soothed his commander with assurances, promises, a kiss of farewell. Word came that the battle was won; England had carried the day. "Thank God – I have done my duty," whispered Nelson.

Not far off, an explosion seemed to rupture the ocean: a French battleship burnt down to its store of gunpowder. Before the splinters of timber had finished rattling down on to the littered sea, Horatio Nelson was dead.

The other casualties were buried at sea, but Nelson was the hero of the hour; he must receive a funeral befitting a saviour of his country. So his little battered and maimed body was put into a barrel, steeped in brandy to preserve it, and guarded night and day by a sailor with a drawn sabre. HMS *Victory* limped home, as mangled by war as Nelson had been, slow to reach harbour and the waiting crowds.

As well as the grand officials, the knights and earls and statesmen who walked behind the flag-draped coffin to St Paul's Cathedral were forty-eight common sailors who had served under Nelson. Weeping openly, those forty-eight were allowed to tear fragments from the flag as keepsakes of their dead commander.

But Emma Hamilton, great love of Nelson's life, was shunned, abandoned to poverty and loneliness. It was as if the nation's tears had blinded them to her very existence.

Fearless, passionate, resourceful and deeply religious, Horatio Nelson joined the British Navy at the age of twelve. He was small – and sickly. He lost the sight of his right eye fighting in Corsica, and later, his right arm at Tenerife. But after winning the battle of the Nile in 1798 and the battle of Copenhagen in 1801, he became the darling of the English public. He died on 21 October 1805 after putting paid to Napoleon Bonaparte's plans to invade England and thus take entire control of Europe. Nelson's Column and Trafalgar Square itself, in which the column stands, are marks of respect to the great naval commander.